High-Quality Leadership

First published 2006 by
Veritas Publications
7/8 Lower Abbey Street
Dublin 1
Ireland
Email publications@veritas.ie
Website www.veritas.ie

10 9 8 7 6 5 4 3 2 1

ISBN 1 85390 942 4

Designed and typeset by Paula Ryan
Printed in the Republic of Ireland by Betaprint, Dublin

Veritas books are printed on paper made from the wood pulp of managed forests. For every tree felled, at least one tree is planted, thereby renewing natural resources.

To my father, Sean Ruth,
my first model of leadership,
courage and integrity

CONTENTS

INTRODUCTION

Participative and collaborative models of leadership are increasingly being adopted in a wide range of educational, pastoral, religious, social, non-profit, community and other settings. A similar trend is evident in the commercial public and private sectors. Some of these are being used in contexts where the traditional or historical model of leadership was one that was largely distant, authoritarian and hierarchical. Increasingly, people who would have been excluded from any significant leadership role are being invited to work collaboratively on leadership teams, pastoral councils, management committees, task forces, partnership groups, steering groups and a range of other collective leadership bodies. This book is aimed at the members of any such leadership teams.

At the same time as new leadership structures and processes are being adopted, there is much confusion about the nature of leadership and what exactly the functions and roles of leaders are. There is also a degree of suspicion and cynicism about the idea of leadership, based, to a large degree, on people's bad experiences with traditional, authoritarian styles of leadership. To add to the confusion and the difficulties, these changes are taking place in what is an increasingly diverse society with a growing recognition of the different needs, backgrounds, identities, interests, experiences and concerns that people bring to their collaborative projects.

In this dynamic and changing environment there are rarely any simple blueprints for success. As leaders, we continually have to monitor and adjust our performance to take account of new circumstances, new challenges and new opportunities. The collaborative process constantly requires us to modify our thinking, question our assumptions, devise new strategies, accommodate new perspectives and remain flexible, creative and innovative in how we approach our tasks.

To be effective and stay on track in such a turbulent and demanding process it helps enormously to step back periodically and assess how we are doing, both individually and collectively. The purpose of this book is to assist 'leaders' to take stock, to identify what they have got right, where they are struggling and how they need to change. The focus is not just on those in very visible, formal leadership positions and with obvious leadership titles but also on those who, *de facto*, sometimes informally and sometimes behind the scenes, are playing clear leadership roles. The type of leadership described in this book is about working collaboratively with other people, trying to influence what happens in order to bring about significant change.

Each chapter contains a short overview of theory dealing with key facets of leadership.[1] The theory in each chapter is followed by a number of practical exercises that focus readers on important elements of their leadership style and effectiveness. These exercises enable each member of the team to assess the strengths and the shortcomings of their own personal approach to leadership as well as understanding how these are shaped by significant aspects of their social identity, their vision and their experience. The exercises also enable the team, as a group, to assess their collective strengths and shortcomings, to identify key issues and challenges facing them, to align what they do with their values and their vision and to invent a range of responses and strategies that will ensure an effective, high-quality leadership.

How to Use this Book

This book can be used in a variety of ways depending on the amount of time available and the particular interest of the individual or group. To begin with, the theory and exercises that follow can be applied as part of an ongoing leadership development programme where the goal is to train and develop new leaders or to strengthen and enhance the effectiveness of existing leaders. By applying the theory and working through the exercises, people can assess the quality of their own leadership, get a much clearer picture of what their role is, as leaders, have greater confidence in their ability to lead and take initiative and identify significant changes and 'next steps' that need to happen for them to become more effective.

Closely related to this, the book can also form the basis of a team-building process to enhance the effectiveness and cohesion of leadership groups. The exercises in each chapter provide a means of identifying team strengths and difficulties as well as a process for devising effective steps to improve their functioning.

The book can also be used as part of a strategic planning process, where individuals and groups use the exercises to strategise and plan how they will make a difference to the people they lead or serve. The questions for reflection guide the team through a process that identifies and clarifies key challenges and workable strategies for responding to them.

More immediately, the exercises in this book can be undertaken in a gradual, chapter-by-chapter process stretching over an extended period of time. Used this way, one or a small number of selected exercises might be completed at regular intervals as a separate part of a longer business meeting. Alternatively, a number of exercises can be built into longer, more dedicated review or development meetings that are scheduled periodically and at which no other business is conducted. In a more comprehensive way still, the exercises can also be used to design a longer training, developmental and self-assessment workshop taking place over a number of days.

In all cases, individual reflection exercises precede the team or group exercises. This is important in assisting people to clarify their own personal thinking, feelings and experience before trying to think about what is happening in their team or in their work. These individual exercises can be done privately and individually on paper; alternatively, they can be done as a dialogue with another individual where they take turns to listen to each other. Some people may find that there is a value in having someone pay attention to them while they think through the various questions and issues. Others may prefer some solitary time to put their thoughts together. In some cases, people may choose to do both. In addition, rather than being done during meetings, many of these individual exercises could also be done as 'homework' prior to meetings, particularly if time is an issue.

The team exercises build on the individual exercises and put considerable emphasis on having people listen well to each other with a minimum of argument or debate. The focus is on helping people to clarify and understand how their colleagues on the team see things and on identifying the key insights and issues that emerge from their discussions. It is particularly important in this context that they are conducted in a non-threatening, non-critical and non-blaming atmosphere. Safety and a relaxed climate will make it easier for people to be both open and honest about their concerns and their struggles around leadership. Particular guidelines for how discussions can be structured to achieve this are given in Chapter 1.

At the end of each chapter, having completed the various exercises, the team is asked to identify three practical steps they will take to follow through on what has emerged from their deliberations. In many cases, there may be more than this but, as a minimum, the team should aim to implement at least three next steps. Finally, exercises related to those in each chapter are indicated at the very end of the chapter. In this way, readers can choose to do exercises that have some similarity or that touch on a common theme. They can also compare their responses in one exercise to how they responded to the related ones.

At the end of this process, individual team members, and the team as a collective, will have a much deeper insight into how they function as leaders as well as greater clarity about the practical steps they can take to offer high-quality, effective leadership. As they progress through the exercises, this growing insight and clarity will be reflected in the quality of their working relationships, the soundness of their thinking about their work and the effectiveness of the decisions they make.

Note

1. A fuller account of this model of leadership is contained in my other book, *Leadership and Liberation: A Psychological Approach* (London: Routledge, 2006).

CHAPTER 1

Leadership and Thinking about People

A central role of leadership is to think about people, about the work and about the situation facing them. This involves being aware of ourselves (our strengths and our struggles), thinking about others (their strengths and their struggles), thinking about the work (what's going well and what's difficult) and thinking about the wider situation (what's happening in the world at large that has implications for us). What is special about high-quality leaders is their ability to think well, or think clearly, about these different aspects. In particular, it is their ability to think 'big' about each of these, to see the whole picture. Everything else they do as leaders rests on the quality of this thinking.

All of this thinking that leaders have to do is also done over the longer term. Not only do we have to be aware of what has happened in the past in regard to each of these elements, we also have to think about the present and what may happen in the future. A challenge for leaders is to take a longer view and to see the bigger picture. This is why having an inspiring vision is often a characteristic of those we admire as great leaders. This high-quality thinking will be reflected in the leader's overall awareness of the situation around them, which we sometimes refer to simply as 'soundness'.

If we are thinking clearly about people, not only will we see their current strengths and the places where they struggle, but we will also see their potential and how they can be supported to become even more effective leaders. Implicit in this central thinking role of leadership is the ability to spot and develop talent. In a very real way, if we did little else as leaders but encourage and support the people around us to see themselves as leaders and take initiative, we would be highly effective and influential. Our leadership would make a significant difference.

Thus, a key role of any leader and any leadership team is to think. The question we face is how sound is our thinking. How clear are we about what's going on around us? Have we got our finger on the pulse of the situation? Can we see where people are struggling? Can we see their potential? As we try to do this, there are these two over-arching questions we are all the time trying to answer: What's going on here? And, what needs to happen?

If we put thinking at the heart of this model of leadership this also means accepting that no one person can possibly hope to do all the thinking for everyone else. If we are to think clearly about any situation we will have to draw on the thinking and experience of the people around us. This, in turn, means recognising that it is not the role of leaders to know all the answers or to be experts. The role of the leader is to facilitate and work through other people to find the answers. This both simplifies the role and helps lift some of the burden of the unrealistic expectations that we sometimes impose on ourselves or other leaders.

If we are to be effective in providing leadership, it is important that we regularly step back to 'take the pulse' of the situation. A danger for some leadership teams is that they get so bogged down in day-to-day problems, fire-fighting or simply administration that they never have enough time to think. A high-quality leadership team will stay connected to and in touch with people. It will also stop every so often to 'check in' with people and take stock of where they have got to and where they need to go next. Thinking is not the only important role for a leadership team but it is a key one. In the chapters that follow we shall examine other significant aspects of this job.

Exercises

Exercise 1.1

Individual Reflection: Me as a Leader

The aim of this exercise is to think about yourself as a leader. There are no right or wrong answers. You may be clearer about some aspects more than others. Notice where you have difficulty answering any of the questions: these may be places where you need more information, where you may need someone to listen to you while you think 'out loud' or where you need to listen to others about what it is like for them.

Alternatively, this exercise may be done in pairs as a mutual listening and sharing of experience.

Think about yourself as someone who plays a leadership role, even if you do not happen to occupy any formal position of leadership or have a leadership title.

1. What are my strengths as a leader? What, in particular, is special or unique about me as a leader or the way I lead? In what ways have I modelled good leadership? How do I make a difference for the people around me?

2. Where is it a struggle for me as a leader? Where has it been hard for me over the past period? What has made it difficult for me to be more energetic, more visible, more committed, more involved, more hopeful and so on? What are the difficult feelings I struggle with?

Exercise 1.2

Step 1 – Team Sharing: Me As A Leader

The aim of this exercise is to get a picture of the strengths and the struggles facing each person as a leader based on their reflections in Exercise 1.1.

Keep the focus on this as a listening exercise and avoid getting side-tracked into any type of intellectual discussion about people's experiences. As you listen, notice the themes that emerge or the issues that get raised repeatedly or echoed in what different people say.

Some detailed guidelines for group discussion are given at the end of this chapter. Keep in mind, for this exercise in particular, the references to confidentiality. In answering the following questions, there are two options: each person in turn may take time to answer both questions together; alternatively, each person may in turn answer the first question and then the second. The latter option takes longer but makes it easier to see the common themes in what people say.

Given the more personal nature of this exercise, finish off by asking everyone to affirm or appreciate another person in the group. For example, ask each person in turn to say one thing they appreciated, respected or admired about the person on their left-hand side. In a smaller team, there might be time for each person to get an appreciation from everyone else in the group.

1. What are my strengths as a leader? What, in particular, is special or unique about me as a leader or the way I lead? In what ways have I modelled good leadership? How do I make a difference for the people around me?

2. Where is it a struggle for me as a leader? Where has it been hard for me over the past period? What has made it difficult for me to be more energetic, more visible, more committed, more involved, more hopeful and so on? What are the difficult feelings I struggle with?

Step 2 – Team Reflection: Implications

Having heard each person talk about their own leadership, the team should now take time to answer the following questions.

It is not necessary that you agree with each other. What is important is that you are clear about what people are saying. (See 'Guidelines for Group Discussion' on page 23.)

1. What struck me most or stood out as I listened to people talking about themselves as leaders?

2. What implications do I think this has for us as a team and how we support each other?

Exercise 1.3

Individual Reflection: The Others on the Team

The aim of this exercise is to step back and think about the other people on the team. This is purely an individual exercise and will not be shared in the wider group.

Think about each of the people on your team individually and what you have heard from them and know of them.

1. What are their particular individual strengths? What leadership potential do they have?

    Team Member A _____

    Team Member B _____

    Team Member C _____

    Team Member D _____

    Team Member E _____

    Team Member F _____

2. What difficult feelings or struggles do I see them facing?

    Team Member A _____

    Team Member B _____

    Team Member C _____

    Team Member D _____

    Team Member E _____

    Team Member F _____

3. How have I been a good support for them individually?

    Team Member A _____

    Team Member B _____

    Team Member C _____

    Team Member D _____

    Team Member E _____

    Team Member F _____

4. Where in particular do I think each of them needs more support?

    Team Member A _____

    Team Member B _____

    Team Member C _____

    Team Member D _____

    Team Member E _____

    Team Member F _____

5. In what particular ways will I support them in the coming period? How will I help them reach their full potential?

    Team Member A _____

    Team Member B _____

    Team Member C _____

    Team Member D _____

    Team Member E _____

    Team Member F _____

Exercise 1.4

Individual Reflection: The Team As A Whole

The aim of this exercise is to think about the team as a whole and how well it functions.

This particular exercise may be done as an individual reflection or in pairs as a mutual listening and sharing of experience.

Think about the team as a whole.

1. In what ways do I think we work well together? What are our strengths as a team?

2. What do I find difficult about the way we work together?

3. What do I think is happening in our group that needs to be addressed as a key issue?

Exercise 1.5

Step 1 – Team Sharing: The Team as a Whole

The aim of this exercise is to get a picture of how each person experiences being a member of the team based on their reflections in Exercise 1.4 above.

Keep the focus on this as a listening exercise and avoid getting side-tracked into any type of intellectual discussion about people's experiences. As you listen, notice the themes that emerge or the issues that are raised repeatedly or are echoed in what different people say.

Keep in mind the 'Guidelines for Group Discussion' on page 23.

1. In what ways do I think we work well together? What are our strengths as a team?

2. What do I personally find difficult about the way we work together?

3. What do I think is happening in our group that needs to be addressed as a key issue?

Step 2 – Team Reflection: Implications

Having heard each person talk about the team as a whole, take time to answer the following questions.

It is not necessary that you agree with each other. What is important is that you are clear about what people are saying. (See 'Guidelines for Group Discussion' on page 23.)

1. What struck me most or stood out as I listened to people talking about the team as a whole?

2. What implications do I think this has for us as a team?

Exercise 1.6

Individual Reflection: The Work

The aim of this exercise is to think about the work of the team and how well it is doing.

This particular exercise may be done as an individual reflection or in pairs as a mutual listening and sharing of experience.

Think about the work you are involved in as a team.

1. What do I think is going well with the work of this team? What successes have we had over the last period? Where do I think we are making progress?

2. What do I see as the difficulties we have faced in relation to this work? What concerns do I have and/or what do I see as key issues for me in relation to this work?

Exercise 1.7

Step 1 – Team Sharing: The Work

The aim of this exercise is to get a picture of how each person thinks about the work of this team based on their reflections in Exercise 1.6.

Keep the focus on this as a listening exercise and avoid getting side-tracked into any type of intellectual discussion about people's experiences. As you listen, notice the themes that emerge or the issues that are raised repeatedly or are echoed in what different people say.

Keep in mind the 'Guidelines for Group Discussion' on page 23.

1. What do I think is going well with the work of this team? What successes have we had over the last period? Where do I think we are making progress?

2. What do I see as the difficulties we have faced in relation to this work?

3. What concerns do I have and/or what do I see as key issues for me in relation to this work?

Step 2 – Team Reflection: Implications

Having heard each person talk about the work of the team, take time to answer the following questions.

It is not necessary that you agree with each other. What is important is that you are clear about what people are saying. (See 'Guidelines for Group Discussion' on page 23.)

1. What struck me most or stood out as I listened to people talking about the work of the team?

2. What implications do I think this has for us as a team?

Exercise 1.8

Individual Reflection: The Wider Situation

The aim of this exercise is to think about the wider situation facing the team in its work.

This particular exercise may be done as an individual reflection or in pairs as a mutual listening and sharing of experience.

Think about the wider situation facing you as a team.

1. What do I see happening currently in the world around us that we, as a team, need to think about?

2. What do I see as the key issues or challenges ahead of us in the coming period?

Exercise 1.9

Step 1 – Team Sharing: The Wider Situation

The aim of this exercise is to get a picture of how each person sees the wider situation based on their reflections in Exercise 1.8.

Keep the focus on this as a listening exercise and avoid getting side-tracked into any type of intellectual discussion about people's experiences. As you listen, notice the themes that emerge or the issues that are raised repeatedly or are echoed in what different people say.

Keep in mind the 'Guidelines for Group Discussion' on page 23.

1. What do I see happening currently in the world around us that we, as a team, need to think about?

2. What do I see as the key issues or challenges ahead of us in the coming period?

Step 2 – Team Reflection: Implications

Having heard each person talk about the wider situation, take time to answer the following questions.

It is not necessary that you agree with each other. What is important is that you are clear about what people are saying. (See 'Guidelines for Group Discussion' on page 23.)

1. What struck me most or stood out as I listened to people talking about the wider situation?

2. What implications do I think this has for us as a team?

Exercise 1.10

Next Steps

Based on what you have heard in these exercises, list three practical steps you will take in this team to improve your ability to keep thinking clearly about yourselves, the work and the wider situation?

1. _____

2. _____

3. _____

Exercises related to those in this chapter appear in Chapters 2, 3, 6, 7, 8, 9, 10 and 13.

Guidelines for Group Discussion

1. **See that everyone gets equal time to talk.**

   To help ensure this, agree a ground rule that no one should speak twice until everyone has had the opportunity to speak at least once. (Individuals may pass on their turn but everyone is given the chance to speak before anyone comes in a second time.)

   Since everyone will get a turn, people can relax and listen without having to worry about interrupting to be heard. This ground rule also means that no one person will dominate the discussion.

2. **Keep the focus on listening and understanding rather than discussion, debate, argument or disagreement.**

   To help ensure this, do not have any discussion until everyone has made their individual contribution. Use this discussion at the end to summarise the key points or issues emerging from the listening.

   By structuring out the discussion after each person's contribution, we make it safer for people to speak and easier for the group to pick up the broad themes and key issues emerging.

3. **Speak from a personal perspective.**

   Encourage each person to speak from their own personal perspective rather than generalising or speaking for others, i.e. their own personal viewpoint, their own personal experiences, their own personal feelings and so on. It is easier to listen to, and harder to disagree with, someone who simply speaks from a personal point of view.

4. **Keep it confidential.**

   Do not discuss what anyone says with people outside the group. Do not refer to anything that is said at a meeting in any way that can identify who said what.

   In relation to sensitive or personal issues, in conversations outside the meeting, do not refer back to what anyone said without, first of all, asking their permission. This is a matter both of courtesy and of safety.

CHAPTER 2

Leadership and Listening

We saw in Chapter 1 how thinking about people is a key role of leaders. We also saw that if leaders are to think clearly about people and the situation facing them, this will require listening deeply and intently to what other people have to say. We know that it is not possible for any one person to do the thinking for everyone else. What is possible is to listen closely to people and use this to clarify our own understanding of the situation. What distinguishes effective, high-quality leaders is their ability to listen well to others and draw on what they hear to make sense of what is going on and what needs to happen.

To get a clear picture of how it is for other people we have to listen on a number of different levels. First, we have to listen to people's *feelings*. Much of the important information in any situation will be communicated at the level of feelings. People will tell us about what they are enjoying or finding fulfilling. They will also tell us about where they are having a hard time or where they are struggling. We face two challenges here. One is to be comfortable listening to feelings, particularly painful feelings, when they emerge. The other is to go after and draw out these feelings by cutting through isolation and making it safe for people to show us their struggle. In any situation, an important question for us is whether or not we can tell what is going well for people and what are the difficult feelings they are struggling with.

Separately from feelings, important information is also communicated through the *stories* people tell us. It helps if we can set things up for people to tell us what their experience has been. Can we listen to what it is like to be this person? Do we have a picture of the kinds of experiences they face, particularly the challenging ones? There is much to be learned from the incidents they describe and the examples they give us.

We also have to listen to people's *thinking*. Sometimes there will be people around us who think very clearly and sharply about the situation, if we are open to hearing what they have to say. What they tell us can make a huge difference to our understanding of what is going on. There will also be other people whose thinking may be confused and intermixed with painful feelings and stories of difficulties. However, if we listen closely enough to each person and widely enough to a range of people, the individual confusion begins to form a pattern that we can make sense of. Gradually, what is confusing to the individual starts to fit into a wider picture that we can see because of the depth and range of the listening we have done. At that point, we can reflect back this wider picture to people in ways that make sense of their confusion.

The only way we are going to get a clear picture of reality is through listening to others. This can take time, although perhaps not as much as we might think. In practice, a lot of the important listening takes place casually, informally and spontaneously or else while we are working together on some other task. Much of it takes place in short bursts or in brief interactions with people. The key challenge is to be able to hear where things are going well and people are pleased with themselves, where they struggle and are having a hard time, and what wisdom and clarity they have gathered as a result of their experiences.

Truly effective leadership is a listening leadership. Evaluating our leadership means examining how much time we spend listening, how well we listen and to whom we listen. This requires great honesty, as few people will admit to being poor listeners (in contrast to the very large number of people who claim they are not being listened to!).

Exercises

Exercise 2.1

Individual Reflection: Listening To Others

The aim of this exercise is to think about how well you listen. There are no right or wrong answers. You may be clearer about some aspects more than others. Notice where you have difficulty answering any of the questions: these may be places where you need more information, where you may need someone to listen to you while you think 'out loud' or where you need to listen to others about what it is like for them.

Think about yourself as someone who plays a leadership role, even if you do not happen to occupy any formal position of leadership.

1. In what ways do I listen well to people who have a different viewpoint, different priorities, different concerns or a different agenda to mine?

2. In what ways do I find it difficult to listen to people who have a different viewpoint, different priorities, different concerns or a different agenda to mine?

3. In relation to the other people on our team or committee, to whom do I have most difficulty listening?

4. In what ways do I react negatively when they speak? What goes on in my head while they speak?

5. What do I think they are trying to communicate even if I have difficulty with the way they do it? What do I think they want people to hear or understand?

6. Various habits can make it difficult for us to hear what someone is saying. On a bad day, which of the following am I inclined to do when listening?

   (a)   Interrupt when I don't agree with or like what I am hearing;
   (b)   Become argumentative – get pulled into an argument that leads nowhere;
   (c)   Get side-tracked into contradicting or correcting any comments that I see as incorrect, inaccurate or untrue;
   (d)   Defend myself against blame or accusations rather than hear the underlying issue or hurt;
   (e)   Blame or accuse the other person and argue over who is right or wrong or who is at fault;
   (f)   Get heated rather than stay calm;
   (g)   Try to score points, win the debate or prove I know better than they do;
   (h)   Respond negatively with sarcastic remarks, patronising comments, criticisms or put-downs;
   (i)   Focus on minor details and miss the underlying message;
   (j)   Carry on an argument in my head while supposedly listening openly;
   (k)   Other (give details).

7. Overall, if I were to be completely honest with myself, what are my greatest shortcomings as a listener?

8. What are three things I will do differently in those conversations I find difficult?

   1. _____

   2. _____

   3. _____

Exercise 2.2

Team Reflection: Listening

The following questions are about listening in your group. Discuss what you see happening without attributing blame to any individual. Keep the focus on listening to what each person thinks rather than arguing with or debating what they say. As you listen to each person, see what consensus emerges or what significant ideas or perspectives find echoes within the group. (See also 'Guidelines for Group Discussion' in Chapter 1 on page 23.)

To begin with, give people time – either on their own or in pairs – to think about each question. Afterwards, go around the group and listen, without comment, to what each person has to say. This can be done over a series of rounds, taking one question at a time and hearing from everyone. If time is an issue, some questions can be combined. Apart from the headings under which they are grouped, they can also be grouped differently: for example, Questions 2, 4, 8, 11 and 13 refer to listening; Questions 1, 7 and 10 refer to supportive factors; Questions 3, 5, 6, 9 and 12 refer to helpful suggestions.

When everyone has had a chance to be listened to, discuss what you see as the main points emerging from this listening.

Listening in the Group

1. In what ways do I think we listen well to each other in this group?

2. When we are not listening well, how do I think this shows itself in the group?

3. Are there people in the group that I would like to hear more from?

4. What do I think gets in the way of everyone having an equal chance to contribute?

5. What would I change to improve the quality of listening in this group?

6. Are there useful ground rules I can think of that would enhance the quality of listening in the group?

Safety

7. In what ways do I think this is a safe group for people to be listened to?

8. In what ways (if any) do I think a lack of safety manifests itself?

9. What do I think would make it even safer?

Painful Feelings

10. In what ways do I think this group is comfortable listening to painful feelings or to the struggles people are facing?

11. In what ways do I think listening to painful feelings or sharing struggles create a difficulty in this group?

Wider Listening

12. Apart from the members of this group, who else do I think we need to listen to in order to enhance our understanding of the wider situation? Where do I think we have not got our finger on the pulse?

13. Who are the groups in this organisation or among the people we serve that I think are often not heard from or listened to?

Exercise 2.3

Next Steps

Based on what you have heard in these exercises, list three practical steps you will take to improve your ability to listen in this group?

1. _____

2. _____

3. _____

Exercises related to those in this chapter appear in Chapters 1, 3, 5, 7, 8, 9, 10, 12 and 13.

CHAPTER 3

Leadership and Relationships

One way to think about leadership is to see it as a process of building close, one-to-one relationships within which we listen deeply to people so that we can think clearly about them.

An important principle is that all effective leadership rests on building solid, one-to-one relationships with people, wherein real work gets done. One way we can measure the effectiveness of our leadership is to examine the quality of the relationships we have built. How connected are we to the people we are trying to lead? If we are not doing the work one-to-one, setting up groups, committees, mass meetings and so on will not compensate for this. However, if we have got this right, these wider forums will be enhanced and more effective.

Building relationships with people involves maintaining close contact with them that is of a high quality. Sometimes, we may not see them that often but, when we do, it makes a difference to them. It is the quality of the contact rather than the quantity of it that counts.

There are a number of things that help to build high-quality relationships. *Listening,* as we saw already, is a hugely important part of the process. Within the relationship, people can tell that they are listened to well and that, in particular, their struggle is understood.

They also get *encouragement* from us not to give up, to have hope and to believe it is possible to make a difference. An important part of leadership is modelling hope in the face of people's doubts, disappointments and disillusionment.

We also build relationships by *affirming people* – by communicating our belief in them, respect for them and our recognition of their abilities and potential. They can tell we like them, respect them, admire them and have high expectations of them.

The other important element in this process is *showing our appreciation* for what they do – regularly and consistently thanking them for their efforts, their help and their initiatives.

All of this is beautifully summed up in the phrase 'catching people doing things right'! We have to shift our focus away from what people do wrong or where they fall short and put it on the things they do right. True leaders have their attention on people's strengths, successes, achievements and potential rather than their weakness, failures, mistakes or shortcomings.

The work of building relationships is a central and ongoing part of leadership. In some groups, attention is paid to relationships only when they break down. That is not workable – a fire-fighting approach will not do. The time to build relationships is when they are in good shape. By working consistently to strengthen our relationships, we can build a solid base of trust and closeness that will sustain us when conflicts emerge, when the organisation is under pressure or when people are struggling with confusion or doubt.

In the end, it is the quality of the relationships we build that will determine how successful we can be in making a difference in the world around us. If we did little else in leadership than focus on building solid, dependable relationships, much of what we hope to achieve would readily fall into place.

Exercises

Exercise 3.1

Individual Reflection: Connections and Closeness

The aim of this exercise is to think about your relationship with others on the team.

This particular exercise may be done as an individual reflection or, alternatively, may be done in pairs as a mutual listening and sharing of experience.

1. In what ways do I feel a sense of connection to others in this group? In what ways do I think we are close to one another?

2. In what ways do I feel isolated in this group? In what ways do I not have a sense of connection to the others?

3. What would make it easier for me to feel more connected or less isolated in this team?

Exercise 3.2

Team Reflection: Connections and Closeness

The aim of this exercise is to get a picture of how each person experiences being a member of the team based on their reflections in Exercise 3.1.

Keep the focus on this as a listening exercise and avoid getting side-tracked into any type of intellectual discussion about people's experiences. As you listen, notice the themes that emerge or the issues that are raised repeatedly or are echoed in what different people say.

Keep in mind the 'Guidelines for Group Discussion' on page 23.

When everyone has had their turn, discuss what you have heard emerging from the listening that you have done.

1. In what ways do I feel a sense of connection to others in this group? In what ways do I think we are close to one another?

2. In what ways do I feel isolated in this group? In what ways do I not have a sense of connection to the others?

3. What would make it easier for me to feel more connected or less isolated in this team?

Exercise 3.3

Individual Reflection: My Relationships with Those We Serve

The aim of this exercise is to think about your relationships with the people you serve or want to serve and your connection to them.

This particular exercise may be done as an individual reflection or in pairs as a mutual listening and sharing of experience.

1. As a leader, with whom do I have solid, one-to-one connections?

2. What is good about my relationships with these people? In what ways am I a positive force in their lives?

3. What are my strengths generally in building close relationships with people?

4. In what ways do I hold back or what is it that gets in my way in building close relationships with people?

5. What are the difficult feelings that I struggle with or that get in my way in building close relationships?

6. What would I do differently in order to build better relationships with the people I want to influence?

Exercise 3.4

Team Reflection: Relationships with Those We Serve

The aim of this exercise is to get a picture of how each person experiences relationships with those the team is serving based on their reflections in Exercise 3.3.

Keep the focus on this as a listening exercise and avoid getting side-tracked into any type of intellectual discussion about people's experiences. As you listen, notice the themes that emerge or the issues that are raised repeatedly or are echoed in what different people say.

Keep in mind the 'Guidelines for Group Discussion' on page 23.

When everyone has had their turn, discuss what you have heard emerging from the listening that you have done.

1. As leaders, where do I think that we as a group have built solid relationships with the people around us?

2. What do I think is good about the quality of the relationships we have built as part of our leadership?

3. In what ways do I think we have not built close relationships with the people around us? Where have we remained isolated in our leadership? Who are the individuals or groups with whom we are less closely connected?

4. For me, what are the difficult feelings that get in my way in building close relationships as a leader?

5. What support do I need to build closer and more solid relationships as a leader?

6. What do I think we, as a group, should do differently in terms of building closer, more solid or more effective relationships?

Exercise 3.5

Next Steps
Based on what you have heard in these exercises, list three practical steps you as a group will take to build better relationships?

1. _____

2. _____

3. _____

Exercises related to those in this chapter appear in Chapters 1, 2, 10 and 13.

CHAPTER 4

Leadership and Vision

As leaders build close relationships and listen to people they get a picture of the strengths, talents and positive attributes of the people they serve. Over time, it is possible to discern a pattern in what we see and hear that allows us to pinpoint some of the things that are special and unique about this group. A key role of leadership is identifying these special qualities.

As we build close relationships and listen and as we create safety for people to communicate with us, as leaders we also get a picture of where they struggle and of the obstacles or barriers they face in their lives. If we pay close attention, these too will emerge as themes or patterns in what we see and hear. Identifying the struggles and difficulties that people face is also a key role of leadership.

As we come to see what is special about people and as we become clearer about their struggle, we are then in a position to clarify our vision. If we enabled and drew forth what is special and if we took on the struggle with hope and power what would happen? If we got it right what would the world look like? A significant piece of our clarity about our vision comes from getting close and listening.

It is also the case that vision arises out of our own lived experience in addition to the connections we build with others. In many cases, the vision is formed early in our lives through formative experiences (and, for this reason, sometimes sounds childish when we try to articulate it). It reflects what matters to us or what is close to our hearts. It is our own personal picture of how we would like to see things different in the world.

Sometimes, the vision is not so much a clearly defined picture of an alternative reality as a clearly enunciated set of core values that will inform and guide us. Some of these are what are called *modal* values, such as fairness, respect and so on, while others are *end* values, such as justice, equality, liberation and so on. The challenge we face is to ensure that our leadership is aligned and consistent with these values. Do we actually practise what we believe in?

At its core, vision is very personal. Connecting with our own personal vision and making it central in our lives and work is much more important than spending a long time as a group trying to come up with an agreed corporate vision. Listening to, and understanding, what each person feels passionately about is more important than crafting a concise statement that summarises all of the individual visions. We have to be wary of substituting bland slogans that differ little from one organisation to another for opportunities for people to regularly connect with the values and vision that are close to their hearts.

People's relationship to their values and their vision varies. For some, the vision is explicit and central to how they lead their lives. For others, the vision is more implicit and not often articulated, while still very important to them. For others still, the vision has become disconnected for one reason or another. In the case of some people, because of the circumstances they found themselves in along the way, they may have got distracted from the vision or been discouraged from pursuing it. Without being hard on ourselves, the reality for some of us may be that we have compromised or become corrupted by the circumstances within which we found ourselves. Regardless of our current relationship to the vision, however, it is the case that, at an emotional level, it still matters to us.

An important part of becoming more effective leaders is taking the time to reconnect with our vision and the core values that underpin it. Any group that wishes to build a shared vision will spend time facilitating people in an ongoing process to connect to their own personal visions. As we listen to one another's dreams, we become inspired by each other and begin to see new possibilities for what is possible and how we can achieve it.

Exercises

Exercise 4.1

Individual Reflection: Values

The aim of this exercise is to think about the values that are important to you in your life.

This particular exercise may be done as an individual reflection or in pairs as a mutual listening and sharing of experience.

1. What are the values that feel important to me? When it comes to the relationships I build, the life choices I make and the way I live my life, what actually matters to me?

2. Thinking of times when I have felt passionate, excited, concerned, bothered, upset or when I had other strong feelings about what I saw happening around me, what do these tell me about what is important to me?

3. What are the important values that I have disconnected from or lost sight of? What used to be close to my heart but for whatever reason I have lost sight of or given up on? What is it I need to reclaim?

4. Thinking of the society around me, what about it gives me hope or energises me?

5. Thinking of the society around me, what disappoints me, discourages me, upsets me or what is it I cannot stand about it?

6. In the light of my answers to the previous questions, what values are central to who I am?

Exercise 4.2

Individual Reflection: Vision

The aim of this exercise is to think about your cherished vision for the future.

This particular exercise may be done as an individual reflection or in pairs as a mutual listening and sharing of experience.

1. Drawing on the values I hold dear, what is my personal vision for the world around me? Describe a future that would inspire me. (If it is hard to connect with a current vision, think back to an earlier time when you did feel connected to a vision and describe that.)

2. In what ways have I tried to realise this vision? What steps have I taken (or am I currently taking) or what strategies have I adopted (or am I currently adopting) to change the world in the direction of my vision? How has this vision influenced the choices I have made or the steps I have taken?

3. If I were to be completely honest with myself, in what ways have I compromised, given up on or failed to pursue my vision and the values that underpin it?

4. If I did not compromise or give up on my vision, what would I do differently? What concrete objectives would I set myself as part of my strategy to achieve this vision?

Exercise 4.3

Team Reflection: Values and Vision

The aim of this exercise is to get a picture of how each person thinks about values and vision in the team based on their reflections in Exercise 4.1 and 4.2.

Keep the focus on this as a listening exercise and avoid getting side-tracked into any type of intellectual discussion about people's experiences. As you listen, notice the themes that emerge or the issues that are raised repeatedly or are echoed in what different people say.

Keep in mind the 'Guidelines for Group Discussion' on page 23.

1. What are the values and the vision that matter to me or are close to my heart?

2. What is my vision for this group and for the people we serve as leaders?

3. In what ways do I think this group has been true to its vision and values?

4. In what ways do I think this group has not been consistent with its vision and values?

Exercise 4.4

Team Reflection: Review and Implications

When everyone has had their turn on the previous exercise, make a list of what you have heard emerging.

1. What important values were highlighted?

2. What aspects of the vision stood out?

3. In what ways do we as a group operate consistently with our values and our vision?

4. In what ways are we out of step with our values and our vision?

5. What steps can we take to align how we operate more consistently with our values and vision?

Exercise 4.5

Next Steps

Based on what you have heard in these exercises, list three practical steps you as a group will take to ensure a better alignment of values, vision and action?

1. _____

2. _____

3. _____

Exercises related to those in this chapter appear in Chapter 10.

CHAPTER 5
Leadership and Decision Making

Leadership teams aspire to adopt a consensus approach to decision making. The process of decision making, however, can sometimes be problematic. In some cases, prolonged indecision, for example, can be highly destructive for the group and its development. Where there is this type of indecision, people's worst qualities often come to the surface in the form of frustration, in-fighting, blaming and hopelessness.

There are a variety of reasons why groups may be indecisive. The absence of consensus on the way forward may lead some groups to postpone decisions until there is full agreement. Sometimes this involves a confusion between consensus and unanimity. In reality, consensus exists where a majority of the group favours a course of action and the other members, while not in agreement with this, are willing to go along with it for the sake of movement or progress, or because they are giving the others the benefit of the doubt. The decision is not so crucial that they would want to hold things up until there is greater clarity or until they have persuaded others to agree with them. Both in spirit and in practice this is different from simple majority rule. Unanimity, however, is where there is total agreement on the way forward. On complex matters this may be quite rare.

At other times, groups may fail to reach agreement because of divisiveness and 'politicking' within the group. A lack of trust makes it difficult for different factions to support one another and instead they oppose whatever it is their rivals propose. This is more likely to occur in situations where people feel threatened and do not have a sense of being listened to or where they cannot tell that their concerns are heard and respected.

Part of the role of leadership is knowing when it is time to act. There comes a point when further discussion will not be helpful and where prolonged indecision may have undesirable consequences. In this situation, the group needs to come to a decision even in the absence of complete agreement. There is a principle that says a group is sometimes better off making a wrong decision than making no decision. If a wrong decision is made, the group can learn from it and try to put it right. If no decision is made, nothing is learned and meanwhile things begin to fall apart. This is particularly the case where decisions are urgent or pressing. In other cases, where the decision is not urgent, where the issue is not hugely important or where maintaining relationships is more important than the issue, a group may decide to postpone a decision to allow time for further discussion, greater clarity and fuller agreement.

The key to reaching consensus and effective decision making is listening. We have to put listening and understanding rather than argument or debate at the centre of our conversations. Where the discussion and decision-making processes are characterised by consistent and ongoing listening it is much easier to reach agreement. Where people can tell that they have been heard and where their issues and concerns are acknowledged and treated with respect, they are less likely to block progress rigidly in the absence of full agreement. Where there is real listening, where people can tell that they do have influence over what happens and where they can tell that the system and the process is not biased against them, they remain flexible around decisions. Where it is clear that a decision is needed, they will not block progress even though they are not in full agreement with what is proposed. Alternatively, they will agree to compromises that allow movement to take place while still leaving room for further discussion.

Occasionally, where consensus is not possible and where decisions are necessary, groups will allow someone in a leadership role to make the decision on their behalf. Having listened to everyone's contribution, this person will be trusted to make their best decision. In the absence of consensus, the group will agree to support whatever decision this person makes and not undermine or attack them if they dislike what they decide. This is workable provided, as we saw above, that people can tell they have been heard, that their thinking is valued and that they do have influence. Mostly, the group will operate by consensus but now and again this option is necessary to ensure that they do not become bogged down in unhelpful or destructive indecision.

Reaching consensus and being decisive can sometimes be messy and conflictual but it is possible as long as we are committed to listening to each other.

Exercises

Exercise 5.1

Individual Reflection: Decision Making

The aim of this exercise is to think about how decisive you are and about your experience of decision making.

This particular exercise may be done as an individual reflection or in pairs as a mutual listening and sharing of experience.

1. What is good about the way I approach decision making?

2. In what ways do I, as an individual, act decisively? In what kinds of situations do I tend to be decisive?

3. In what ways do I, as an individual, procrastinate or act indecisively? In what kinds of situations do I find it hard to be decisive?

4. What have been the best experiences of decision making I have witnessed in any group?

5. What have been the worst experiences of decision making I have witnessed in any group?

6. In what ways could I change in order to be more effective in discussion and decision-making situations?

Exercise 5.2

Step 1 – Team Reflection: Group Decision Making

The aim of this exercise is to get a picture of how each person experiences the decision-making process in the team based on their reflections in Exercise 5.1.

Keep the focus on this as a listening exercise and avoid getting side-tracked into any type of intellectual discussion about people's experiences. As you listen, notice the themes that emerge or the issues that are raised repeatedly or are echoed in what different people say.

Keep in mind the 'Guidelines for Group Discussion' on page 23.

What is Positive about our Decision Making?

1. What do I think is good about the way we make decisions in this group? In general, what have we got right about this process?

2. In what ways do I think we, as a group, have modelled decisive leadership?

3. What do I think is good about the ways we have handled disagreements and a lack of consensus?

4. To what extent do I, as a member of this team, feel heard and respected when we are not in agreement on issues?

5. From my point of view, in what ways have we, as a group, maintained good relationships in spite of any disagreements over decisions?

Concerns about our Decision Making

1. What concerns do I have about the way we make decisions in this group?

2. In what ways do I think we as a group have acted indecisively?

3. What do I think is difficult about the way we have handled disagreements and a lack of consensus?

4. To what extent do I, as a member of this team, feel I have not been fully heard and respected when we are not in agreement on issues?

5. From my point of view, in what ways, if any, have our relationships in this group been affected negatively by disagreements over decisions?

What we could Do Differently?

1. How do I think we, as a group, could have handled more effectively situations where there was a lack of agreement?

2. What practical steps do I think we could take to improve the decision-making process in this group?

Step 2 – Team Reflection: Review of Key Points

Once each person in the group has spoken about decision making, take time to answer the following questions about the key points emerging.

It is not necessary that you agree with each other. What is important is that you are clear about what people are saying. (See 'Guidelines for Group Discussion' on page 23.)

1. What positive things stood out from what you heard?

2. What important concerns were highlighted?

3. What possibilities for improvement stood out?

Exercise 5.3

Next Steps

Based on what you have heard in these exercises, list three practical steps you as a group will take to ensure a more effective decision-making process in the future?

1. _____

2. _____

3. _____

Exercises related to those in this chapter appear in Chapters 2, 8, 9 and 13.

CHAPTER 6

Leadership, Authority and Authoritarianism

Some people are uncomfortable with the idea of having leaders. It can conjure up images of an oppressive or abusive use of power. Many people have had bad experiences with people in positions of power or authority, whether in the family, in school, in the Church, in the community or in their work. These bad experiences can lead people to assume that all leadership is inherently abusive or oppressive. However, there is confusion here between a number of related but different concepts and it is important to clarify these differences.

To begin with, we can make a distinction between leadership and authority. By its nature, leadership is something we *take* and something we do. For example, it is a decision we make to see that what happens around us goes well. It is not something we need permission for. We just take it. This is different from authority, which is something we *are given* and a position that we occupy. We are elected or appointed to this position of authority. In practice, leadership and authority may, or may not, coincide. It is possible to lead without having authority and it is possible to exercise authority without taking leadership. Ideally, however, where we have authority we would also take leadership and when this happens in practice, the person in authority relies very little on the power or trappings of authority to get things done. They influence people through their leadership rather than command them through their authority. They do not use their authority to control people or impose their thinking on them and are very comfortable delegating to other people. Their concern is with achieving results rather than who gets credit for them.

Where authority is not accompanied by leadership, the person in authority tends to become authoritarian. Unable to influence people through leadership, they fall back on their authority to command or require people to do things. They then emphasise rules and regulations, and insist on the recognition of, and respect for, their authority. Quite often, in this situation, they become reluctant to delegate or to trust people to take initiative or think for themselves. In the extreme, they become punitive, over-controlling, disempowering and oppressive.

Thus, leadership in itself is not a problem. There is nothing inherently oppressive or abusive about leadership. It is actually a necessary function in any group and the greater the number of people who take it the better things go. Similarly, giving people authority is not in itself a problem. In some situations it makes sense to give people the authority to make certain decisions or to speak on behalf of a group (with the assumption that they will also exercise leadership in carrying out this role). The problem is not with leadership or authority. The problem is with authoritarianism – authority divorced from leadership.

The challenge we face is to take full leadership in any situation. More particularly, where we are given authority, the challenge is also to take leadership. Even though I have been given formal authority, I have to make a personal decision to act as a leader. The challenge also is to recognise when authority has become divorced from leadership. Much of the cynicism and distrust that characterises many people's relationship with those in positions of authority and leadership is actually due to authoritarian power-wielding detached from any element of true leadership.

In a high-quality leadership team, any formal authority coincides with leadership and the relationships are characterised by mutual influence rather than one-way, hierarchical command and control. Leadership is cherished as a positive resource rather than being viewed suspiciously and the group is committed to enhancing the initiative and influence of each individual.

Exercises

Exercise 6.1

Individual Reflection: Authority, Authoritarianism and Leadership

The aim of this exercise is to think about your experiences around people in authority positions and the effects they have had on you.

This particular exercise may be done as an individual reflection or in pairs as a mutual listening and sharing of experience.

1. Think about the people in formal positions of authority that I dealt with growing up (for example teachers, school principals, priests/ministers, police, social workers and so on). Which of these stand out as having had a positive effect on me or built a positive relationship with me?

2. What was it about the people I thought of that enabled them to have this positive effect on me or to build this positive relationship with me? What were the qualities or characteristics of these people or what was it they did that influenced me so positively?

3. Think about the people in formal positions of authority that I dealt with growing up (for example teachers, school principals, priests/ministers, police, social workers and so on). Which of these stand out as having had a negative effect on me or built a negative relationship with me?

4. What was it about the people I thought of that caused them to have this negative effect on me or to build this negative relationship with me? What were the qualities or characteristics of these people or what was it they did that influenced me so negatively?

5. In what ways (if any) do negative feelings about authority or authoritarianism in general influence how I view or exercise formal authority?

6. In what ways (if any) do negative feelings about authority or authoritarianism in general influence how I view or exercise leadership of any kind?

Exercise 6.2

Step 1 – Team Sharing: Authority and Authoritarianism

The aim of this exercise is to get a picture of each person's experiences of authority and authoritarianism based on their reflections in Exercise 6.1.

Keep the focus on this as a listening exercise and avoid getting side-tracked into any type of intellectual discussion about people's experiences. As you listen, notice the themes that emerge or the issues that are raised repeatedly or are echoed in what different people say.

Keep in mind the 'Guidelines for Group Discussion' on page 23.

1. What were the qualities, characteristics or behaviour of the people in authority who positively influenced me?

2. In what ways did they manifest leadership while occupying a position of authority?

3. What were the qualities, characteristics or behaviour of the people in authority who negatively influenced me (i.e. authoritarians)?

4. In what ways did they not manifest leadership while occupying a position of authority?

5. In what ways (if any) do negative feelings about authority or authoritarianism in general influence how I view or exercise formal authority?

6. In what ways (if any) do negative feelings about authority or authoritarianism in general influence how I view or exercise leadership of any kind?

Step 2 – Team Reflection: Lessons

When everyone has had their turn on the previous questions, take time to answer the following questions about the key lessons emerging.

It is not necessary that you agree with each other. What is important is that you are clear about what people are saying. (See 'Guidelines for Group Discussion' on page 23).

1. What are the lessons from this about the positive or constructive exercise of formal authority?

2. What are the lessons from this about the negative or destructive exercise of formal authority (i.e. authoritarianism)?

Exercise 6.3

Team Reflection: Authority and Leadership in the Team

With a clear picture of the differences between leadership, authority and authoritarianism, the aim of this exercise is to think about authority and leadership in this group.

This exercise can be done as a series of rounds, hearing from each person individually, in line with the guidelines for group discussion. Alternatively, it can be done in the form of a brainstorming session, listing various responses on a flip chart.

1. What formal authority (if any) has this group been given?

2. How has our exercise of this authority coincided with the exercise of leadership by this group?

3. In what ways (if any) has our exercise of authority become divorced from leadership and taken on elements of authoritarianism?

4. What formal authority (if any) has been given to any particular member(s) of this group?

5. How has this person's exercise of authority coincided with the exercise of leadership by them?

6. In what ways (if any) has their exercise of authority become divorced from leadership and taken on elements of authoritarianism?

7. In what ways (if any) do negative feelings about authority or authoritarianism in general influence how we in this group view or use our authority?

8. In what ways (if any) do negative feelings about authority or authoritarianism in general influence how we in this group exercise leadership?

9. Given all we have heard, what would we change or do differently to ensure a more positive, constructive or effective exercise of authority and leadership?

Exercise 6.4

Next Steps

Based on what you have heard in these exercises, list three practical steps you as a group will take to ensure a positive, constructive and effective exercise of authority and leadership?

1. _____

2. _____

3. _____

Exercises related to those in this chapter appear in Chapters 1, 5 and 11.

CHAPTER 7

Leadership and Oppression

Leadership does not operate in a vacuum. There is a social context within which we lead and a set of lived experiences that we bring to leadership. These experiences have shaped, and continue to shape, how we think, feel and act. In particular, a core element of this social context is the experience of oppression that takes a heavy toll on people, both individually and collectively. We carry the 'baggage' from this experience into our relationships and into our leadership.

To be truly effective in leadership we need to understand and be aware of the ways in which oppression affects us and the people we serve. As a leader, I need to be aware of the ways in which I personally have experienced oppression and how those experiences have affected me – physically, emotionally, socially, spiritually, economically and so on. My awareness of my own experience of oppression plays a key role in enabling me to empathise with, and empower, other people. I can see how my oppression has left me feeling bad about myself and my people, how it has interfered with my relationships, how it has undermined my ability to take initiative and take leadership, along with the other destructive effects of this experience. My struggle to overcome these effects and to eliminate the oppression in my own life becomes a key source of inspiration about, insight into and understanding of the struggles of other people. My journey towards liberation engages me in the same struggle as the people I try to serve and ensures that our relationship becomes one of mutual liberation rather than an unequal, unbalanced or oppressive helping relationship in which the onus is primarily on the other person to change.

As well as becoming aware of my own oppression and working towards my own liberation, it makes a huge difference to the quality of leadership I can offer if I am committed to raising my awareness of other people's experiences of oppression. Leaders who make a difference have their fingers on the pulse of the people they serve. They understand their struggles and the effects that oppression has on them. At the same time, they do not confuse the effects of the oppression with what is inherently true of people as humans.

We now know that most of the damage done by oppression is done when it becomes internalised within the person and within the group. Over time, oppression distorts the ways in which people think, feel and act. This *internalised oppression* is reflected in characteristic ways whereby people in a group feel bad about themselves and their people (such as low self-esteem, shame, feelings of inferiority and so on). We can see it in the characteristic ways they feel powerless and hopeless around taking action to bring about change. It shows up in the characteristic ways that divisiveness, in-fighting and isolation permeate their relationships and make it difficult for them to unite and cooperate with each other. Sometimes it can be seen in the characteristic ways they engage in harmful or self-destructive behaviour (such as high rates of suicide or the abuse of alcohol or drugs). Often, it emerges in the way their own feelings of victimisation pull people into competing with, mistreating or oppressing the members of other marginalised groups that we might expect to be their natural allies. Essentially, internalised oppression disconnects people from a sense of their inherent goodness and worth and replaces this with a grossly distorted picture of themselves and the world around them. As leaders and allies, the challenge for us is not to confuse the various effects of the oppression with what is actually true of people inherently. We see the struggle but we never lose sight of the person underneath that struggle.

Effective, high-quality leadership is grounded in an awareness of how oppression operates. This awareness informs our thinking about the work we do and the people we serve. Leading in this way means that, when it comes to what it is like to be a member of an oppressed group, we 'get it' much more than other people who are outside that group. Our awareness enables us to become very effective allies for those who are marginalised, underprivileged, disadvantaged, treated unjustly or oppressed.

Exercises

Exercise 7.1

Individual Reflection: Oppressed Experiences

The aim of this exercise is to think about your experiences of being oppressed and the effects they have had on you.

This particular exercise may be done as an individual reflection or in pairs as a mutual listening and sharing of experience.

1. In what ways have I experienced oppression in my life? What were the formative experiences of hurt or mistreatment during my life that have adversely affected the ways I now think, feel or act?

2. For each of these formative experiences, how, in particular, did they leave me feeling about myself and the world around me? What painful feelings was I left with?

3. In spite of these hurtful experiences, what aspects of my inherent humanity have I managed to hang on to or stay connected to (for example a sense of worth, love, courage, power, goodness and so on)?

4. If I were to go against any messages or painful feelings that I internalised because of my experience of oppression and if I were to move proudly and powerfully in the direction of complete liberation from oppression, what would I do differently or what steps would I take?

Exercise 7.2

This is a practical exercise that can be taken on as a project. The aim is to build a relationship with someone from another oppressed group and learn about their experiences of being oppressed.

Reach out to, make friends and build a warm connection with a member of another oppressed group. When it seems appropriate, invite them to share with you some of the details of their own experience of oppression and their struggle for liberation.

Listen with interest to their story, paying particular attention to what they internalised and to the painful feelings these experiences left them with.

The questions in Exercise 7.1 can be a guide to this conversation with them.

Exercise 7.3

Step 1 – Team Sharing: Oppression and Its Effects

The aim of this exercise is to get a picture of the struggle facing each person and the journey towards liberation that they are engaged in.

Keep the focus on this as a listening exercise and avoid getting side-tracked into any type of intellectual discussion about people's experiences. As you listen, notice the themes that emerge or the issues that get raised repeatedly or are echoed in what different people say.

Keep in mind the 'Guidelines for Group Discussion' in Chapter 1 (page 23), in particular the references to confidentiality.

Given the more personal nature of this exercise, finish off by asking everyone to affirm or appreciate another person in the group. For example, each person in turn can give an appreciation of the person on their left-hand side. In a small group, there might be time for each person to get an appreciation from everyone else in the group.

1. In what ways have I experienced oppression in my life? What were the formative experiences of hurt or mistreatment during my life that have adversely affected the ways I now think, feel or act?

2. For each of these formative experiences, how in particular did they leave me feeling about myself and the world around me? What painful feelings was I left with?

3. In spite of these hurtful experiences, what aspects of my inherent humanity have I managed to hang on to or stay connected with (for example a sense of worth, love, courage, power, goodness and so on)?

4. If I were to go against any messages or painful feelings that I internalised because of my experience of oppression and if I were to move proudly and powerfully in the direction of complete liberation from oppression, what would I do differently or what steps would I take?

Step 2 – Team Reflection: Implications

Once each person in the group has spoken about their experiences of oppression, take time to answer the following questions about the key points emerging.

It is not necessary that you agree with each other. What is important is that you are clear about what people are saying. (See 'Guidelines for Group Discussion' on page 23.)

1. What struck me most or stood out as I listened to people talk about their experiences of oppression?

2. What implications does what they have said have for this team and its work?

Exercise 7.4

Next Steps

Based on what you have heard in these exercises, list three practical steps you as a group will take to raise awareness around oppression and/or to ensure that policy, practice and the work of this group reflects an awareness of the existence and operation of oppression.

1. _____

2. _____

3. _____

Exercises related to those in this chapter appear in Chapters 1, 2, 8 and 9.

CHAPTER 8

Leadership and Identity

Individuals do not have just one social identity. We are a mix of different identities – gender, class (for example working class, middle class), nationality (for example Irish, British, Nigerian, Romanian, French), ethnic (for example, Black, White, Traveller), religious (for example Catholic, Protestant, Jewish, Muslim), sexual orientation (for example heterosexual, gay, lesbian, bisexual, transgender), age (for example young person, young adult, elder), family (for example parent, child, sibling) and so on. Some of these are oppressed identities and some oppressor. Not only am I likely to have experienced oppression in my life, I will also have experienced privilege, power or dominance to some degree. Some of these oppressed and oppressor identities have more salience or significance in my life than others. Some of them are salient because my experiences within these identities have had a profound effect or influence in my life so far. Others are salient because they relate to important relationships that I have now or want to build in the future.

At first glance, I may not seem to have a lot of feelings attached to these latter identities but the people I want to relate to may have experienced hurt or mistreatment at the hands of other people who share the same identity as me. For that reason, this identity has a potentially significant influence on our relationship. For example, many White people do not think of themselves as White, as having a White identity. They are not aware of any strong feelings attached to being White. However, if I, as a White person, want to build a close relationship with a Black person, then this identity takes on a lot of importance in that context.

I have other identities that apply to me but they were not the source of as much hurt or oppression or they did not involve particularly positive experiences that have stayed with me. Neither are they significant in terms of the relationships I am involved in at present. Thus, these latter identities are more peripheral to who I am. This could, and might well, change as the range and diversity of my relationships expand. For now, however, I can probably identify a handful of core identities that are central to me and my relationships and a wider group that I experience as secondary and more peripheral.

The quality of my leadership and my relationships will tend to reflect my level of awareness of both the oppressed *and* the oppressor identities that I occupy. Do I know what my key identities are? Am I aware of the identities I bring into my relationships? Am I aware of what people with these identities internalise and struggle with? Do I know how different identities affect the type of leadership people take? For example, it is relatively easy for people with oppressor identities to take up leadership positions. As members of an oppressor group, we may have managed to retain a greater level of confidence in ourselves, our thinking or our opinions. We may not feel as intimidated by being visible as others might or we may be more comfortable in positions of authority. Because of our conditioning, unless we are committed to raising our awareness of how oppressor patterns operate, we may end up undermining the leadership of oppressed people or usurping leadership positions that could more usefully be filled by members of an oppressed group. This is a crucial issue for leaders in 'helping' or 'caring' professions and for groups and individuals that are committed to being allies for members of oppressed groups. In a similar way, as members of an oppressed group, we may struggle with feelings of inadequacy or lack of confidence that make us reluctant to take on visible leadership roles or fearful of speaking out or upsetting people. An awareness of the source of these struggles and a commitment not to collude with what we have internalised, can enable us to act powerfully in spite of any pull to stay silent or invisible. It allows us to see the problem as the oppressive system rather than a personal failing.

For leadership teams, an awareness of the dynamics of identity enables us to locate and address a range of problems and issues that might otherwise remain invisible or result in people being misdiagnosed as 'problem people'.

An effective, high-quality leadership team will see issues of identity as central to how well they function. It will create the space and the safety for people with different identities to be visible, to be heard from, to be thought about and to be supported while also confronting any oppressiveness that might interfere with their relationships.

Exercises

Exercise 8.1

Individual Reflection: Oppressed Identities

The aim of this exercise is to think about the range of oppressed identities that you belong to and the effects that being a member of these groups has had on you. (This builds on the exercises in Chapter 7.)

Here you are asked to name your oppressed identities. This refers not only to those identities within which you have felt mistreated but also to those that, within the society or culture, actually occupy positions of low power, low status, low privilege or inequality, regardless of whether or not you have felt mistreated.

This may be done as an individual reflection or in pairs as a mutual listening and sharing of experience.

1. What are the main oppressed groups to which I belong or have belonged? (For example, think in terms of areas such as gender, age, class, race, ethnicity, disability, religion, nationality, culture, sexual orientation and so on.)

2. Which of these oppressed identities have been most significant in terms of the effects they had on me?

3. In relation to each of my significant oppressed identities, what was positive about being a member of that group? (For example, what positive aspects of my humanity have I, or people who share this identity, been able to hang on to or have a connection to, such as sense of humour, sense of fun, sense of community, spontaneity, ability to love, courage, pride and so on?)

4. How, in particular, have I experienced hurt or mistreatment as a member of each of these oppressed groups?

5. How did that experience of hurt or mistreatment leave me feeling about myself and about people who share the same identity as me? (For example, in what ways have I internalised doubts about myself or my people, shame or a difficulty in taking pride in myself or people like me, hopelessness, powerlessness, isolation, anger and so on?)

6. In what ways do I continue to struggle, emotionally or otherwise, as a result of the hurt or mistreatment I experienced?

Exercise 8.2

Individual Reflection: Oppressor Identities

The aim of this exercise is to think about the range of oppressor identities that you belong to and the effects that being a member of these groups has had on you.

Here you are asked to name your oppressor identities. This refers not only to those identities within which you have felt dominant, oppressive or privileged but also to those that, within the society or culture, actually occupy positions of power, high status, privilege or unequal advantages (regardless of whether you have felt oppressive or not).

Like many of the exercises in this book, this one requires you to be as honest as you can be with yourself. Naming your oppressor identities is not something you may find easy. Naming these identities does not mean you are a bad person or that you intend to mistreat or oppress other people. It simply means that you have been born into, or acquired, the identity of a group that, within the society or culture, occupies a position of power or privilege. In other words, you have this identity regardless of how you treat other people.

This may be done as an individual reflection or as a mutual listening and sharing of experience.

1. What are the main privileged or oppressor groups to which I belong or have belonged? (For example, think in terms of areas such as gender, age, class, race, ethnicity, disability, religion, nationality, culture, sexual orientation and so on.)

2. Which of these oppressor identities have been most significant in terms of the effects they had on me?

3. In relation to each of my significant oppressor identities, how have my experiences of power or privilege left me feeling about myself (positively and/or negatively) as a member of this group and about other people with this same identity?

4. In relation to each of my significant oppressor identities, in what ways have my experiences of power or privilege had a positive effect on my relationships with members of the equivalent oppressed group? How have I been a good ally for them?

5. In relation to each of my significant oppressor identities, in what ways have my experiences of power or privilege had a negative effect on my relationships with members of the equivalent oppressed group?

6. In relation to each of my significant oppressor identities, in what ways have I held back from supporting, getting close to or otherwise being an effective ally for members of the equivalent oppressed group?

7. If I were to be a more effective ally for members of particular oppressed groups, what would I do differently?

Exercise 8.3

Team Reflection: Oppressed and Oppressor Identities

The aim of this exercise is to get a picture of the mix of identities represented in this group and the effects that this has within the group.

Keep the focus on this as a listening exercise and avoid getting side-tracked into any type of intellectual discussion about people's experiences. As you listen, notice the themes that emerge or the issues that are raised repeatedly or are echoed in what different people say. Keep in mind the 'Guidelines for Group Discussion' on page 23.

The first four questions are largely a collating of what people have learned from the previous exercises. The final three questions are about the implications of this for the group.

Given the more personal nature of this exercise, finish off by asking everyone to affirm or appreciate another person in the group. For example, each person in turn could give an appreciation of the person on their left-hand side. In a small group, there might be time for each person to get an appreciation from everyone else in the group.

1. What are the significant oppressed identities represented in this group? (Make a list.)

2. In what ways do these oppressed identities affect how people with those identities think, feel or act in this group?

3. What are the significant privileged or oppressor identities represented in this group? (Make a list.)

4. In what ways do these oppressor identities affect how people with those identities think, feel or act in this group?

5. What do I think is positive about the mix of oppressed and oppressor identities in this group?

6. What difficulties have I noticed as a result of the particular mix of oppressed and oppressor identities in this group?

7. What are the key themes or challenges that have emerged as we listened to one another?

Exercise 8.4

Next Steps
Based on what you have heard in these exercises, list three practical steps you, as a group, will take to raise awareness of the different identities in this group, of different identities in the community you serve and to increase the visibility, safety and leadership of members of oppressed identity groups?

1. _____

2. _____

3. _____

Exercises related to those in this chapter appear in Chapters 1, 2, 7 and 9.

CHAPTER 9
Leadership and Diversity

In most situations, the people and groups we lead are not homogeneous. As we have seen, they are a mix of different social identities, among them many oppressed identities and some oppressor identities. In thinking about people, it is important to do this not just about them as individual personalities but also about them as members of these various oppressed or oppressor groups. Many of the conflicts and difficulties we have to deal with will be infused, or intertwined, with oppressed/oppressor dynamics. We are trying to think about, mobilise and organise diverse constituencies with different experiences, different struggles, different needs and different resources. Often we are trying to build some sense of unity and collaborative process across what may be very divisive relationships, low levels of trust, varying degrees of hope about the possibility of change, low levels of awareness of others' feelings and experiences, varying degrees of empowerment and varying degrees of connectedness and closeness.

The level of awareness around the diversity of the group will differ depending on, among other things, the general level of awareness in the culture. So, for example, there may be greater awareness in many groups around issues to do with gender equality, at the very least to the extent of having some discussion about it if not some concrete action. There is likely to be less awareness around issues to do with classism, racism, 'adultism' or sexual orientation, for example. There may indeed be some identities that are kept invisible and never discussed or where there is very little safety for people to express their needs or make any demands. Within this process, we can expect that some subgroups or constituencies will feel overlooked, ignored, misrepresented, misunderstood or mistreated.

The challenge we face in leadership is to cherish and nurture diversity. If we are thinking well about people and their development, we will want to draw on the full person with all the richness that they bring to the situation from their diverse experiences and backgrounds. We will not require them to leave important chunks of their identity and their humanity at the door as they enter. We will want to address anything that gets in the way of their being fully involved with us or that prevents them using all their talent and strengths. This means making it safe for people to claim their identity and be visible with that identity. They are here not just as an individual but as a person who is female, or Black, or an elder, or a young person, or an immigrant, or gay, or a Traveller, or has a disability and so on. Our awareness in this group about these various identities will affect the safety and the support we provide and the effectiveness of the leadership we offer.

Evaluating our leadership then means assessing how well we deal with diversity. How sensitive are we to cultural, social and other differences? How culturally competent are we? To what extent do our policies, procedures, practices, values and vision reflect a welcoming, nurturing and acceptance of diversity?

One principle that has emerged in relation to diversity is that in order to nurture diversity we have to acknowledge the different identities that are present. Going a step further, the way to build unity across diversity is for these different identities to meet separately at least some of the time. By creating a safe place for people to meet on their own to share common experiences and think together, we can make it more likely that people will be open to listening to and supporting others with different identities.

Exercises

Exercise 9.1

Individual Reflection: Reactions to Diversity

The aim of this exercise is to think about your reactions to people whose identity is different from yours.

This may be done as an individual reflection or in pairs as a mutual listening and sharing of experience.

In doing this particular exercise, an important focus is on being completely honest with yourself. The aim is to try to see the reality of your situation rather than they way you think it should be. So, if the truth were told …

1. In what ways am I a good ally or support for people whose identity is different from mine? (For example, in relation to gender, class, race, ethnic background, nationality, age, disability, sexual orientation and so on.)

2. In what ways am I uncomfortable with, unaware of, isolated from, scared of, awkward around or otherwise negative towards people whose identity is different from mine? (For example, in relation to gender, class, race, ethnic background, nationality, age, disability, sexual orientation and so on.)

3. What negative messages or stereotypes did I experience in relation to any of these other oppressed groups? (For example, when growing up, what messages did I get about Black people, Travellers, poor people, working-class people and so on?)

4. Even though, at an intellectual level, I may know that such messages and stereotypes are not true or accurate, at an emotional level how do they still have a hold on me and on the way I think about or behave around members of these groups?

Exercise 9.2

Team Reflection: Openness to Diversity

The aim of this exercise is to think together about the range of diversity among the people we are trying to lead or serve and how we can be more open and supportive to them.

Keep the focus on this as a listening exercise and avoid getting side-tracked into any type of intellectual discussion about people's experiences. As you listen, notice the themes that emerge or the issues that are raised repeatedly or are echoed in what different people say.

Keep in mind the 'Guidelines for Group Discussion' in Chapter 1 (page 23) in particular the references to confidentiality.

1. What are the oppressed identities represented among the people we are trying to lead or serve? (Make a list.)

2. What are the dominant or oppressor identities represented among the people we are trying to lead or serve? (Make a list.)

3. Which of these various identities are most visible, have most voice and are most represented in leadership roles generally? Whose needs are most met in what we do?

4. Which of these various identities are least visible, least heard from and least represented in leadership roles generally? Whose needs are least met in what we do?

5. What oppressed identities in the community we serve are not represented, or are under-represented, in this group?

6. What feelings, experiences or struggles faced by those who are currently not represented here (or under-represented) might make it difficult for them to be part of this group?

7. Think of possible reasons why this group might not be a safe or welcoming place for those who are currently not represented (or under-represented) here.

8. What opportunities exist for people (in this group or in the wider community) who share the same identity to meet on their own, to listen to one another, share experiences and think about and identify their needs?

9. What opportunities exist for people with diverse identities (in this group or in the wider community) to come together to listen to one another, learn about each other's experiences and struggles, and think about how to be effective allies for one another?

10. In what ways is our response to diversity consistent or inconsistent with our values and vision?

11. If our group truly welcomed, nurtured and celebrated diversity, what would we do differently?

Exercise 9.3

Next Steps

Based on what you have heard in these exercises, list three practical steps you as a group will take to make this group more responsive to diversity and more welcoming and safe for people who are different.

1. _____

2. _____

3. _____

Exercises related to those in this chapter appear in Chapters 1, 2, 7 and 8.

CHAPTER 10
Leadership and Strategising

We can think of any group as being composed of people with varying degrees of commitment, satisfaction, awareness, influence and potential. While everyone has the potential to act as a leader, at any given point, some people are in better shape than others to take greater initiative and leadership. Some have the potential to play a more influential role at this point. Some are relatively stuck or unable to play much of a constructive role for one reason or another.

In particular, we can think of three categories of people who make up the group or organisation as a whole. The first of these is composed of people who are enthusiastic about the work, highly committed, energetic, positive and supportive. They are great to have around and make a big difference in any situation. Unfortunately, in many situations, people such as this may be in the minority.

There is a second, much larger category of people who are interested, reasonably committed and broadly supportive. They are open to change if they can see its value. They are willing to help if they can but are not necessarily very enthusiastic or energetic. They may have other priorities, other concerns or commitments, and may not see our issues or our agenda as of central importance for them. While not against us, they may not be totally sold on our vision or convinced about the way forward. Some of them may disagree with what we are doing but they are not inflexible or destructive in the ways they communicate. This middle group will often be the largest of the three categories.

People in the third category are quite different. Commonly they are upset, disaffected, suspicious or angry. They do not like what we are doing. They fight us all the way. Their approach tends to be blocking and very destructive, either indirectly sabotaging or attacking and undermining. Often, they feel hard-done-by, mistreated and misunderstood. Their style can be abrasive and confrontational. They can be difficult to be around and are often preoccupied with giving out about all that they see as wrong. Quite often they become isolated and have a way of gravitating towards other people who feel equally upset. Where the overall morale of a group is low they can have quite an influence and can make it difficult for any real progress to be made. This is the category that we tend to lose sleep over and that often soaks up much of our attention. In general, however, this tends to be a relatively small number of people, sometimes only one or two in any group.

From a leadership perspective, the key question is where to put our energy. In a group or organisation with each of these categories of people, where does it make sense to focus? How can we be most effective faced with these different types of people? How can we bring about change under these conditions? Well, we already have the support and commitment of the first category so it makes sense to stay close to and maintain our connection with these people. With the third category, we are unlikely to make much progress, at least in the short term. Chance is unlikely to come from that direction. This is not to suggest that we should ignore these people but simply that we do not waste our energy trying to bring them around to our way of thinking. The place where we can make the biggest difference is with the second category. People here are open to change if we choose to go after them and build relationships of influence. Many of these have the potential to play key leadership roles if they get the encouragement and support that they need. Because they do not cause any trouble, it can be easy to ignore them or overlook them and focus instead on the difficult third category. Putting our energy into this second category, however, has the greatest potential to transform situations. By strengthening and empowering people in the second category, we can significantly reduce the relative influence, and the negative impact, of those in the third category.

The challenge is to be strategic in how we think about these various relationships. Effective leaders strategise where they will put their energy and direct their efforts.

Exercises

Exercise 10.1

Individual Reflection: Personal Connections

The aim of this exercise is to think about and strategise your relationships.

This is an individual strategising exercise. It is not for sharing or discussion with the people concerned. The purpose of it is to assist you to think about your relationships with the people around you and to plan specific actions you might take to develop these relationships.

1. To whom am I closely connected in this group of leaders? (To whom am I close? With whom do I get on well or have a good relationship? Who do I like or enjoy?)

2. To whom am I not as closely connected in this group of leaders? (With whom have I not spent much time? About whom do I not know much? To whom have I not spoken in a long time?)

3. To whom am I not close at all in this group of leaders? (Around whom do I find it hard to be? Who do I find difficult? About whom do I worry or fear?)

4. Who are the people in this group with the potential to play an even greater leadership role? Who has the potential to make a difference here?

5. In relation to these people with potential, what specific steps could I take to strengthen my relationship with them and to support and encourage their development?

6. If I were to take steps to become a person of greater influence in this group, what would I do differently in relation to each of these relationships? (Which relationships would it make sense to put my energy into and how would I do it? List the specific steps you would take in relation to each of the relationships you have highlighted.)

Exercise 10.2

Team Reflection: Strategising

The aim of this exercise is to think about and strategise relationships. In Exercise 10.1 the emphasis was on thinking about other people on the team. Here the emphasis is on the people this team is trying to serve.

Keep the focus on this as a listening exercise and avoid getting side-tracked into any type of intellectual discussion about people's experiences. As you listen, notice the themes that emerge or the issues that get raised repeatedly or are echoed in what different people say.

Keep in mind the 'Guidelines for Group Discussion' on page 23.

1. Who are key leaders, key people of influence or key people that make a difference around them as I see it in the community we serve?

2. In what specific ways do I think we can support these key people more and build on their potential?

3. Who are other people with the potential to make a difference or to play a greater leadership role as I see it in the community we serve?

4. In what specific ways do I think we can support them more and build on their potential?

5. To whom do I think we are not well connected in the community we serve? (Who have we not spent enough time with or listened to enough? With whom have we lost touch? For whom do we not have our finger on the pulse?)

6. In what specific ways do I think we can build a better relationship with them, support them more and build on their potential?

Exercise 10.3

Team Reflection: Goal Setting

The aim of this exercise is to make suggestions and propose specific goals for this group in the coming year.

As a team, take time to hear from each person on the following questions. These questions overlap somewhat but they allow people to think about the work of the group from slightly different perspectives.

As before, keep the focus on this as a listening exercise and avoid getting side-tracked into any type of intellectual discussion about people's experiences. As you listen, notice the themes that emerge or the issues that are raised repeatedly or are echoed in what different people say.

Keep in mind the 'Guidelines for Group Discussion' on page 23.

1. If this group were to be very strategic in the coming period, where do I think should we put our energy and what should we do differently?

2. Given the values and vision that were articulated in Chapter 4, the strategising in Exercise 10.2 and the suggestions people put forward in answer to the last question, what specific goals would I propose for the work of this group in the coming year? (List these on a flip chart.)

Exercise 10.4

Team Reflection: Prioritising

The aim of this exercise is to rank the goals proposed in Exercise 10.3 in order of priority.

Take the list of proposed goals from Exercise 10.3 and prioritise them using a system of weighted voting, as follows.

1. Give each individual three slips of paper.

2. Ask them to pick three of the goals on the list and rank them in order of preference.

3. Ask them to write each of these preferences on a separate slip of paper, clearly indicating what rank they assigned them.

4. Gather the set of first preferences. Each of these is assigned 3 points. Do a tally to see the total points for each of these goals.

5. Gather the set of second preferences. Each of these is assigned 2 points. Do a tally to see the total points for each of these goals.

6. Gather the set of third preferences. Each of these is assigned 1 point. Do a tally to see the total points for each of these goals.

7. On the flip chart, record the total number of points for each goal.

8. The goals can now be ranked in order of priority using these points. The highest points represent the overall first choice of the group.

9. Decide on a cut-off point for goals. For example, it often happens that the first number of items on the list are relatively close together in terms of the points they receive. Further down the list, there may be a marked gap between the points for one particular item and the points for the next item in succession. This could be taken as a cut-off point. The items above this point will be the key goals for the coming period in the order of priority that emerged.

10. Alternatively, the group may simply decide to take the three or four highest-ranking goals on the list and concentrate on these.

Exercise 10.5

Next Steps
Based on the strategies and goals highlighted by the group, list three practical next steps in the process of implementing these strategies and goals.

1. _____

2. _____

3. _____

Exercises related to those in this chapter appear in Chapters 1, 2, 3, 4, 11 and 13.

CHAPTER 11

Leadership, Isolation and Attacks

Organisations and groups sometimes put considerable effort into ensuring that the best people are put into leadership roles. Much care is taken to select people who will make a positive contribution and bring much-needed skills to the role. One of the challenges faced by groups is to ensure that leaders who are selected actually thrive and survive once they take on that role. In particular, groups have to think about how they can support leaders, particularly when they are struggling in the role, making mistakes or under pressure. When difficulties emerge, there can be a tendency for groups to settle for being upset at leaders rather than thinking carefully about how best to support them. This can lead to a situation where the person in a leadership role becomes isolated or feels under attack. At such times, much of their energy then goes into surviving and watching their back rather than into high-quality leadership.

Reactions to leaders tend to fall towards one or other of two extremes. When people are upset with the leader, they can react passively by ignoring them, avoiding them, not communicating with them, not listening to them, leaving them on their own, not giving them any help, not giving them any positive feedback, not supporting them, showing little appreciation for their efforts, giving no encouragement, adopting a negative attitude towards them or showing little commitment to them. Essentially, they isolate and abandon the leader. Alternatively, they may react more actively by attacking them, being hostile or abusively critical towards them, publicly criticising them, complaining about them to others, gossiping about them, threatening them, ostracising them, refusing to cooperate with them or bypassing them in the chain of command.

In most cases, these passive and active reactions are experienced as destructive. They do little to assist the leader to overcome any difficulties and make it harder for them to think clearly about what makes sense. Over time, if these reactions persist, they can become institutionalised and the norm for how leadership difficulties are addressed. At this point, the solution adopted by the group for poor or unsatisfactory leadership, as they see it, is to 'do in' the leader. As a result, many people emerge from leadership roles feeling very bruised and hurt by the ways they were treated by those around them. They feel shocked and let down by the way people responded to their leadership.

To develop effective leadership, it is important that groups address the issue of support for leaders. People function well and effectively when they feel supported and well thought about. They do not function well in isolation or under attack. Isolating or attacking leaders is not a workable way to ensure good leadership.

Faced with leadership that is in difficulty or not functioning the way we would like it to, the challenge is to *think* actively about the person in the leadership role rather than settling for being upset with them. The challenge is to notice where they may have become isolated and take steps to break through that isolation; notice where they may be under attack and take steps to interrupt that process; think about the person in that role and how best we can support them to function well under difficult circumstances. Effective teams do not abandon leaders when they falter.

Exercises

Exercise 11.1

Individual Reflection: Reactions to My Leadership

The aim of this exercise is to think about your experiences of helpful and unhelpful reactions from other people to your leadership.

This may be done as an individual reflection or in pairs as a mutual listening and sharing of experience.

1. When I think about leadership situations where I have functioned well, the kinds of support from other people that I found helpful included the following ... (Make a list of things other people did or ways they responded that you found positive or constructive.)

2. When I think about leadership situations where I found it difficult or where I struggled, the kinds of reactions from other people that I did not find helpful included the following ... (Make a list of things other people did or ways they responded that you found negative or destructive.)

3. How was I affected emotionally by the difficulties and negative reactions I encountered?

4. How was I affected physically (for example eating, sleeping, health and so on) by the difficulties and negative reactions I encountered?

5. How was my behaviour and my leadership affected by the difficulties and negative reactions I encountered?

Exercise 11.2

Team Reflection: Support for Leaders

The aim of this exercise is to think about how better to support people who are leading.

Keep the focus on this as a listening exercise and avoid getting side-tracked into any type of intellectual discussion about people's experiences. As you listen, notice the themes that emerge or the issues that are raised repeatedly or are echoed in what different people say.

Keep in mind the 'Guidelines for Group Discussion' in Chapter 1 on page 23.

1. In what ways do I think we are good at supporting each other's leadership in this group?

2. What other positive steps do I think we could take to support each other's leadership?

3. What are the kinds of reactions that, as I see it, are not helpful for someone in a leadership role?

4. Which of these do I think we need to be particularly alert to in this group?

Exercise 11.3

Brainstorming: Ground Rules

The aim of this exercise is to generate a list of useful ground rules for assisting people who are in difficulty, struggling or having a hard time in leadership.

Brainstorming is a technique to gather as many ideas as possible, before deciding which ones to discuss in depth. It avoids a common mistake of spending too much time discussing the first suggestion offered so that not enough time is left to discuss other and perhaps better suggestions.

Based on the discussion in Exercise 11.2, the brainstorming should be done by drawing one suggestion at a time from each group member and recording these on a flip chart. All ideas, no matter how absurd or wild, should be encouraged.

Generating a list of possibilities is the first step. Afterwards, these can be discussed in some depth for clarification and assessment of their workability. Comments and discussion on individual points should not be allowed, however, until all the suggestions have been collected.

1. As a group, brainstorm a list of strategies, ground rules or 'dos and don'ts' for dealing with someone who is in difficulty, having a hard time or struggling in a leadership role. (These may include positive and constructive actions that could be taken along with negative or destructive actions to be avoided.)

2. Having brainstormed the list, discuss the ones you consider most important and workable, most supportive or most useful for dealing with leadership difficulties.

Exercise 11.4

Team Reflection: Prioritising

The aim of this exercise is to rank the suggested ground rules in order of priority.

Take the list of suggestions from Exercise 11.3 and prioritise them using a system of weighted voting, as follows:

1. Give each individual three slips of paper.

2. Ask them to pick three of the suggestions on the list and rank them in order of preference.

3. Ask them to write each of these preferences on a separate slip of paper, clearly indicating what rank they assigned them.

4. Gather the set of first preferences. Each of these is assigned 3 points. Do a tally to see the total points for each of these suggestions.

5. Gather the set of second preferences. Each of these is assigned 2 points. Do a tally to see the total points for each of these suggestions.

6. Gather the set of third preferences. Each of these is assigned 1 point. Do a tally to see the total points for each of these suggestions.

7. On the flip chart, record the total number of points for each suggestion.

8. The suggestions can now be ranked in order of priority using these points. The highest points represent the overall first choice of the group.

9. Decide on a cut-off point for suggestions. For example, it often happens that the first number of items on the list are relatively close together in terms of the points they receive. Further down the list, there may be a marked gap between the points for one particular item and the points for the next item in succession. This could be taken as a cut-off point. The items above this point will be the key ground rules for the coming period.

10. Alternatively, the group may simply decide to take the highest-ranking suggestions on the list and concentrate on these.

Exercise 11.5

Next Steps
Based on the suggestions highlighted by the group, list three practical next steps in the process of supporting leaders over the coming period.

1._____

2._____

3._____

Exercises related to those in this chapter appear in Chapters 6, 10 and 12.

CHAPTER 12

Leadership and Conflict Resolution

Dealing with conflict is a normal part of leadership. As we tackle potentially emotive or divisive issues, as we attempt to move in ways that challenge taken-for-granted assumptions or ways of doing things, as we develop more culturally and socially diverse memberships or as we confront issues of identity and liberation, we are likely to experience conflict along the way. This does not mean that something has necessarily gone wrong. It may be simply a reflection of the complexity of issues, the presence of strongly held viewpoints or the existence of deeply felt emotions. If it is handled well it can enhance the creativity and effectiveness of the group. Handled badly, it can lead to demoralisation and an inability to explore fully and resolve problems or issues.

As leaders we may be called on to handle people's upsets and difficulties with one another or with us. We may find ourselves having to deal with difficult one-to-one conflicts where another person is upset, disruptive, challenging, attacking or generally behaving in ways that are inappropriate. We may also find ourselves in situations where the difficulties we confront are within a group with, perhaps, a number of people having trouble coping with each other. Sometimes the conflict will involve us directly and sometimes we will be in the role of a third party trying to mediate and help other people to resolve their differences.

In conflict situations, we know that a number of things make it difficult for people to be effective. One of these is that, under stress, people's thinking shuts down. It becomes difficult for them to think clearly or to come up with creative ways of resolving the difficulty they face. A second is that, under stress, people's judgement gets distorted and they have difficulty accurately assessing what is facing them. They may misinterpret what is said or misread the body language. They may see criticism or threats where none are intended. Under these circumstances, people fall back on a more primitive response and rely on unthinking, habitual ways of dealing with the situation that are rigid, inflexible and inappropriate. Often, the ways they react when under stress and shut down are a rigid re-enactment of old habits from the past that they used when they felt threatened in other situations.

Their inability to think clearly and their lack of judgement mean that they make no allowances for how this situation is different from these past situations and thus could be dealt with differently.

A key skill in situations such as these is the ability to stay calm in the face of other people's upsets. The challenge is to stay thinking clearly and not simply sink into our own fears, worries, anger and so on. Our feelings are not a good guide to how we should react. Rather, our reaction has to be based on what makes sense rationally in the situation rather than what we feel like doing.

A number of considerations enter into any discussion of conflict resolution. One is the quality of listening. It has been said that it is possible to listen people into agreement much more easily than to argue them into agreement. As an individual, am I able to listen and see the real person underneath the upset? Can I hear what the person is saying, separately from any unhelpful ways they may be saying it? In terms of the group, to what extent are discussions characterised by real listening as opposed to destructive argument, debate or point scoring. Are all viewpoints explored? Are differences treated with respect? Are divergent approaches seen as enhancing the group's effectiveness? Is the focus on understanding what people are saying rather than disagreeing with them? Similarly, is the group process one that assists people to listen and communicate or does it permit destructive patterns to impede good communication.

In a high-quality leadership team, conflict is managed effectively and constructively. There is an openness to people's feelings and to divergent points of view, good listening, clear understanding of what is said, very little point scoring or rigid argumentation, and a full exploration of issues that arise. There are also periodic reviews of how well they are functioning in relation to conflict.

Exercises

Exercise 12.1

Individual Reflection: Reactions to Conflict

The aim of this exercise is to examine your own personal style of dealing with conflict.

This may be done as an individual reflection or in pairs as a mutual listening and sharing of experience.

Complete the following sentences:

1. When someone is actively hostile towards me (critical, angry, threatening, abusive etc.), on a good day I tend to react by ...

2. When someone is actively hostile towards me (critical, angry, threatening, abusive etc.), on a bad day I tend to react by ...

3. People close to me say that when I am in a difficult conflict situation I tend to ...

4. If the truth were told, I usually react to negative criticism by ...

5. When things are not going well in a relationship that I value, I tend to react by ...

Exercise 12.2

Individual Reflection: Strengths and Weaknesses around Conflict

The aim of this exercise is to identify your strengths and weaknesses in dealing with conflict and the changes you need to make.

This may be done as an individual reflection or in pairs as a mutual listening and sharing of experience.

Based on your responses to the statements in Exercise 12.1, summarise here your overall approach to dealing with conflict.

1. My greatest strength in handling difficult or conflict situations with other people is ...

2. My greatest weakness in handling difficult or conflict situations with other people is ...

3. Overall, my way of dealing with interpersonal conflict is to ...

4. The thing I need to learn to do in these situations is ...

Exercise 12.3

Step 1 – Team Reflection: Dealing with Conflict and Differences

The aim of this exercise is to survey the members of the group to assess how they judge the group's ability to deal with conflict and differences.

The following survey items can be completed individually and anonymously by group members and the results collated for later discussion by the group. The aim is to pinpoint any aspects of the group's functioning about which people have some concerns.

Alternatively, each item can be discussed by the group as a whole and areas of concern highlighted. The aim of this exercise is not to blame or point fingers but to focus on any areas where the functioning of the group can be made more effective.

Survey of Group Process I

For each of the following statements, tick the box that best describes how you see things. The final statement gives you an opportunity to make additional comments.

1. People in this group feel free to express their opinions, viewpoints and feelings.

1. Never	2. Rarely	3. Sometimes	4. Usually	5. Always

2. Each person is listened to openly and with respect.

1. Never	2. Rarely	3. Sometimes	4. Usually	5. Always

3. One or two people dominate or monopolise discussions.

1. Never	2. Rarely	3. Sometimes	4. Usually	5. Always

4. Issues are fully explored and all important aspects are aired.

1. Never	2. Rarely	3. Sometimes	4. Usually	5. Always

5. I have confidence in the group's ability to resolve differences and conflicts.

1. Never	2. Rarely	3. Sometimes	4. Usually	5. Always

6. Conflicts become personalised.

1. Never	2. Rarely	3. Sometimes	4. Usually	5. Always

7. There is an openness to how people feel about issues as well as to what they think about them.

1. Never	2. Rarely	3. Sometimes	4. Usually	5. Always

8. Discussions in this group are characterised by significant efforts to clarify positions and viewpoints rather than merely arguing, disagreeing over or debating points.

1. Never	2. Rarely	3. Sometimes	4. Usually	5. Always

9. There is a marked divergence between what people say informally, outside of meetings, and what they say in the meetings.

1. Never	2. Rarely	3. Sometimes	4. Usually	5. Always

10. Members play a constructive role during meetings.

1. Never	2. Rarely	3. Sometimes	4. Usually	5. Always

11. Reporting of meetings is accurate and free of controversy.

1. Never	2. Rarely	3. Sometimes	4. Usually	5. Always

12. There are taboo subjects or issues in this group.

1. Never	2. Rarely	3. Sometimes	4. Usually	5. Always

13. Concerns I have about how conflict and differences are dealt with, which have not already been raised, include the following …

Step 2 – Team Reflection: Implications

Having surveyed the members of the team, take time to answer the following questions about the key points emerging.

It is not necessary that you agree with each other. What is important is that you are clear about what people are saying. (See 'Guidelines for Group Discussion' on page 23.)

1. What struck me most or stood out as I listened to people talk about what they see happening in the group?

2. What implications do what was said have for this team and how we operate?

Exercise 12.4

Next Steps

Based on the issues highlighted by the group, list three practical next steps the team will take to improve the way conflict is dealt with in the coming period.

1. _____

2. _____

3. _____

Exercises related to those in this chapter appear in Chapters 2, 11 and 13.

CHAPTER 13

Leadership and Problem Solving

Leadership teams are often presented with complex problems that have persisted over long periods or that have defied earlier attempts to devise workable solutions. There are a number of guidelines that help to clarify the nature of difficulties in the way of resolving such problems. Sometimes, where groups have failed to solve pressing problems, it is because they have been talking at cross-purposes. They have not made a clear distinction between discussions of positions, discussions of solutions and discussions of demands, and they have not identified how these are different from discussions of problems. For any complex or emotive issue, if the discussion remains at the level of discussing the positions people have taken up or the solutions they favour or the demands they are making, it is highly unlikely that agreement will be reached. To achieve agreement, there is a need for communication on a deeper level.

Part of the role of leadership is to think about what is being said and to notice whether or not people are all talking about the same thing or at cross-purposes. It sometimes happens that different solutions argue with each other without their proponents ever agreeing on the nature of the problem. At other times, people simply take up opposing positions, dig their heels in and never find any common ground. Or they make what seem like impossible demands without making it clear what their concerns are or what interests are at stake. Leaders can play an important role by helping to focus the discussion in ways that pinpoint the real problems, identify common concerns, highlight important interests, reveal key issues or clarify principled stands.

Symptoms of inadequate problem-solving processes are when stalemate occurs or where the same problem recurs in spite of repeated efforts to deal with it. Usually, these are signs that important elements of the problem have been missed or misunderstood. Key questions are whether or not the real problem has been identified, whether or not it is clear what the underlying interests are, whether or not all people's concerns have been clearly voiced, whether or not there are fears or other feelings behind what people are saying, whether or not all the issues have been raised and whether or not there are important principles at stake. Without knowing all of these it can be extremely difficult to reach agreement on the way forward.

Moving a discussion to a deeper level involves a combination of interested questions and respectful listening. By repeatedly asking for clarification, asking why something is important to the other person, why they see things the way they do, how they see something can be done, what concerns they have in the situation and so on, we can gradually uncover the full complexity of the problem. By listening respectfully to what people have to say we can find ways to 're-frame' the problem in terms of these underlying concerns, interests, feelings, principles and so on. What is presented as a solution can be re-framed in terms of the underlying problem. What is presented as a position can be re-framed in terms of an underlying interest or concern. If we listen well and re-frame accurately, there will be ready agreement with what we say. Once the issue is re-framed in ways that everyone accepts, it is then possible to look for alternative means of meeting the widest range of needs in the situation.

Even where an individual's preferred solution is not adopted, there will often be an agreement to go along with other people's ideas. Once people can tell that they have been heard and taken seriously, there is an openness to being flexible and a willingness to keep the process moving rather than block progress.

Exercises

Exercise 13.1

Individual Reflection: Problem Solving

The aim of this exercise is to step back and think about how effective the group is at addressing issues and solving problems.

This may be done as an individual reflection or in pairs as a mutual listening and sharing of experience.

Complete the following sentences:

1. What I am pleased with about this group and the way it has functioned so far in addressing issues or problems is ...

2. Where I think we have not functioned well in addressing issues or problems is ...

3. Key issues or problems in relation to our work that I think we need to address are ...

4. Key issues or problems in relation to our efficiency and effectiveness as a group that we need to address are ...

Exercise 13.2

Step 1 – Team Reflection: Problem Solving

The aim of this exercise is to survey the members of the group to assess how they judge the group's ability to tackle issues and solve problems.

The following survey items can be completed individually and anonymously by group members and the results collated for later discussion by the group. The aim is to pinpoint any aspects of the group's functioning about which people have some concerns.

Alternatively, each item can be discussed by the group as a whole and areas of concern highlighted. The aim of this exercise is not to blame or point fingers but to focus on any areas where the functioning of the group can be made more effective.

Survey of Group Process II

For each of the following statements, tick the box that best describes how you see things. The final statement gives you an opportunity to make additional comments.

1. Problems keep recurring in spite of repeated attempts to resolve them.

1. Never	2. Rarely	3. Sometimes	4. Usually	5. Always

2. There is clear agreement on the nature and scope of problems before solutions are proposed or discussed.

1. Never	2. Rarely	3. Sometimes	4. Usually	5. Always

3. Issues and problems ar explored in depth by this group rather than treated in a rushed or superficial way.

1. Never	2. Rarely	3. Sometimes	4. Usually	5. Always

4. Meetings of this group are efficient.

1. Never	2. Rarely	3. Sometimes	4. Usually	5. Always

5. Agendas reflect the real issues, concerns and brief of this group and its members.

1. Never	2. Rarely	3. Sometimes	4. Usually	5. Always

6. Agendas are covered fully in the course of meetings.

1. Never	2. Rarely	3. Sometimes	4. Usually	5. Always

7. The purpose of discussions in this group are clear to all members.

1. Never	2. Rarely	3. Sometimes	4. Usually	5. Always

8. Discussions in this group are characterised by respectful listening and clarification of what people are saying.

1. Never	2. Rarely	3. Sometimes	4. Usually	5. Always

9. The group works by consensus.

1. Never	2. Rarely	3. Sometimes	4. Usually	5. Always

10. The group is effective at decision making.

1. Never	2. Rarely	3. Sometimes	4. Usually	5. Always

11. Group members play a constructive role in problem solving.

1. Never	2. Rarely	3. Sometimes	4. Usually	5. Always

12. Being a member of this group is fulfilling for me.

1. Never	2. Rarely	3. Sometimes	4. Usually	5. Always

13. Concerns I have about how this group solves problems, which have not already been raised, include the following …

Step 2 – Team Reflection: Implications

Having surveyed the members of the team, take time to answer the following questions about the key points emerging.

It is not necessary that you agree with each other. What is important is that you are clear about what people are saying. (See 'Guidelines for Group Discussion' on page 23.)

1. What struck me most or stood out as I listened to people talk about what they see happening in the group?

2. What implications does what was said have for this team and how we operate?

Exercise 13.3

Next Steps

Based on the issues highlighted by the group, list three practical next steps to improve the functioning of the group in the coming period.

1. _____

2. _____

3. _____

Exercises related to those in this chapter appear in Chapters 1, 2, 3, 5, 10 and 12.